OPEN *to* BEHOLD

Seeing God in Everyday Nature

THIS BOOK IS A GIFT

from the author

Slight flaws in a print run gave me the opportunity to donate this book.

To order a new book:

www.ThereseBachHeyek.com

or 1-800-342-3782 ERVA Publications

OPEN *to* BEHOLD

Seeing God in Everyday Nature

Photographs and Reflections by Therese Bach Heyek

For Erwin, who has believed in me since I was nineteen, has
loved me through our twenty-five years of marriage, and who encouraged
me to put this book into print. I am in awe of your love.

www.theresebachheyek.com

Erva Publications
3100 West Grand Avenue
Chicago, Illinois 60622
ISBN: 978-0-615-38448-1
ISBN: 061538448X

First Edition 2010

Cover and layout design – Amy Carnaghi
Photograph editor – Carol Freeman
Book editor – Mary Clare Goller

Border image reprinted by permission of Shutterstock Images LLC.
Printed in China

INTRODUCTION

Warm sunlight, cool sparkling water, the smell of the earth after a rain… God woos us through nature. Nature's colors, movement, texture, fragrance and melodies get our attention and invite us to a deeper awareness of God.

To illustrate, one morning a puddle on our driveway captivated me. Autumn leaves rested on the thin puddle—and in the puddle was a reflection of the tree the leaves fell from. The leaves and the tree, now separated, were united again from this different perspective. I felt like I was given a glimpse into our mystical world where there is more going on than we know. I went in to get my camera to capture the mystery found in a puddle (p. 79).

On another occasion, driving through southeast Wisconsin, I noticed a solitary tree growing in a field. I unexpectedly felt drawn to it—something about its strength and the way it was anchored in the earth led me into reflection. I took a photograph as we passed by (p. 63).

We all have moments like these when we are stopped in our tracks by a breathtaking sunset or the wind blowing through the leaves. In this book, I hope to share the myriad of possibilities in everyday nature to be led into deeper contemplation—contemplation about nature, ourselves and God.

Joyce Rupp devotes a chapter on "far-seeing eyes" in her book, *The Star in My Heart.* She encourages us to use and develop our intuitive ability to bring us into deeper contemplation. The simplicity and beauty that is present in nature can help move us to another way of seeing. Joyce's words gave me greater confidence to trust in my experience, as I now invite you to do!

Contemplating nature, we may see qualities of God, just as art reveals an artist. What we each perceive in nature will vary, and what we may notice one day will differ the next. Nature is always changing so a person may gaze at the same tree day after day and there will always be something new to see. I take each walk full of eager anticipation of what I might discover in a new way about God.

Nature helps me to see God physically at work. The rhythm, growth, and change of nature speak to me of a living God – one who continues to create in our midst. Through nature - through the air we breathe and the food we eat - God faithfully sustains, nourishes and physically loves us.

I am grateful to nature. Most often, nature is an easy companion, a gentle teacher. Nature is always available, ready to show us something, freely. Wherever we are, there is always a tree, a view of the sky (if from a window), a plant (if in the room), or a bird to give our attention to. Nature is always busy growing, flying, living, and dying, but not too busy to share of itself.

I invite you to use this book to become more aware of God's presence in nature all around you. Be open to behold!

Mine eyes were opened to behold all hidden things... —Christina Rosetti

ACKNOWLEDGEMENTS

I have been blessed with incredible support from family and friends through the five years of envisioning this book to getting it into print. They are all part of its creation. To these supportive people I am particularly grateful:

My husband, Erwin, who listened when it was just a vision in my heart, encouraged me to work on it, empowered me with a new camera lens, and then shared in countless conversations.

My friend, Julie Berggren, who loved my photographs, challenged me to polish my writing style with her good literary advice, and shared generously of her experience in book publishing, introducing me to a book designer and book editor. Julie is the muse for the title.

My friend, Jennifer Grant, who loved the pages from the start, supported me through many versions, shared her wisdom, and was more eager than I to see it in print!

My friend, Dorian Merrick, who listened and offered her wisdom over countless coffees, was solid ground for me during a difficult time, and was proud of me through it all.

My book designer, Amy Carnaghi, who creatively and beautifully designed the book's present form. I am indebted.

My photo editor, Carol Freeman, who reviewed my early photographs and encouraged me, then generously offered her fine eye to edit the photographs in this book. See Carol's amazing photographs of nature at **carolfreemanphotography.com.** Her work is an inspiration to me.

My book editor, Mary Clare Goller, who made excellent suggestions, shaping my work with her smart sense of words, just in time!

Joyce Rupp, whose books inspire me, and who generously gave me confidence with her words of praise.

Last, but not least, our German shepherd, Wolfy, whose desire for a daily walk pushed me out the door! I now know the beauty in rain, ice, and fog because she took me out in it, and then patiently waited when I stopped to photograph.

Apprehend God in all things,

for God is in all things.

Every single creature is full of God

and is a book about God.

Every creature is a word of God.

If I spent enough time with the tiniest creature—

even a caterpillar—

I would never have to prepare a sermon.

So full of God is every creature.

—Meister Eckhart

❋ S P R I N G ❋

Spring's warmth beckons

dormant buds to blossom.

Your love awakens us,

inviting us to new life.

The color blue

gives cause for joy.

In each sunlit flower

Your love is visible.

Tree buds,

    full of life, open.

Each new leaf unfolding,

    bears witness to Your life-giving presence.

Drops of rain

  hold life.

Your power, although vast,

  is held in a single drop of rain.

A sticky net is

ready for catching.

You instill in us resourcefulness.

May we use our gifts.

A cloud changes in appearance,
yet still is a cloud.

May we be open to all variations
of Your presence on earth.

Leaves of an ancient species

grow anew.

You create new life

throughout time.

Perfectly sized,

    a robin's nest serves well.

Your meticulous care

    perfectly suits us.

Despite its wounds,

   a tree steadfastly lives.

You heal us so we may grow

   graciously with our wounds.

A spring rain

    refreshes all living things.

You satisfy us

    in physical ways.

A small blossom

captures our attention.

Even the tiniest things

inspire awe of You.

Each leaf contributes

  to the tree's grandeur.

We are all part of something

 much greater than ourselves.

 We are all part of You.

May it be my custom to go outdoors each day

among the trees and grasses,

among all growing things

and there may I be alone,

and enter into prayer

to talk with the one that I belong to.

—Rabbi Nachman of Bratzlaw

❀ S U M M E R ❀

Radiant hues

   signal a new day.

You give us new beginnings,

   continuously.

A ghost crab scurries by

hardly noticeable.

We recognize Your presence

when attentive.

Shades of emerald

   glow in the sun's light.

You illuminate us

   as You reveal Yourself through us.

Led by hidden light,

    a bee finds nectar.

You guide us

    in ways unseen.

A lake greets

   each raindrop.

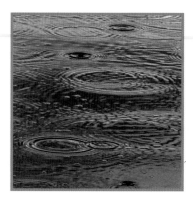

You respond to us

   individually.

A rock, amid foliage,

serves by simply being.

May we learn to be

as profoundly present

to You and others.

The surf pushes,

    and the undertow pulls.

You urge us above and beneath

    the surface of our awareness.

DYNAMIC GOD

Parched, cracked

    earth waits for rain.

Your love flows through

    every crevice of our being.

A tree grows beyond

  initial boundaries.

Your dynamic Spirit

  cannot be contained.

A carpet of common clover

offers nourishment.

Your goodness

is in all of creation.

GOD WHO UPLIFTS

Willow branches

lift in a breeze.

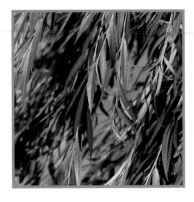

Your Spirit

exhilarates us.

Evening's fading light
cannot be slowed by
our desire for another hour.

Acknowledging our powerlessness,
we receive Your timelessness.

When you find a place in Nature

where the mind and heart find rest,

then you have discovered

a sanctuary for your soul.

—John O'Donohue

❀ A U T U M N ❀

Tender leaves hold

potential to be

a mighty tree.

You have given us

everything

from the beginning.

GOD WHO ANCHORS

A solitary tree grows strong,

connected to the earth.

You call each of us to be

firmly rooted in You.

Whittled timber

shows industriousness.

You celebrate

our accomplishments.

A golden canopy

reaches for light.

Your love attracts us to You.

Autumn leaves reveal

    their underlying colors.

You are with us throughout

    our ongoing transformation.

An encircling vine adorns

its companion tree.

With Your grace,

those we embrace enrich us.

Lightly flowing water

    smoothes stone.

You shape us with

    Your constant, gentle love.

Resplendent leaves fall

in their time.

May we trust in You,

and let go.

A tree hollow serves others

as a safe haven.

Your love creates good

from the hardships we bear.

Leaves and tree, now separated,

meet again in a puddle.

A puddle offers a glimpse

into Your mystery.

Countless milkweed seeds
take flight.

You grace us with abundant
opportunities in life.

Sunlight breaks through

hindering fog.

Your loving Spirit

penetrates our darkness.

To be of the Earth is to know

    the restlessness of being a seed

    the darkness of being planted

    the struggles toward the light

    the pain of growth into the light

    the joy of bursting and bearing fruit

    the love of being food for someone

    the scattering of your seeds

    the decay of the seasons

    the mystery of death

    and the miracle of birth.

—John Soos

❀ W I N T E R ❀

Broken ice is

  shaped by proximity.

Through our close relationships,
Your Spirit forms us.

Rough layers unfold,

uncovering inner softness.

Becoming open,

Your heart speaks to ours.

Exquisite designs

form on a windowpane.

Your artistry—intricate

yet playful—excites us.

A soft snow highlights

distinctive lines.

You bring out our qualities

with Your gentle presence.

Ice gems spray

onto shore.

Your power exerts itself

in dramatic ways.

Coneflowers wait

for summer.

You give us hope that

love will rise again.

Winter wind

    sculpts sand.

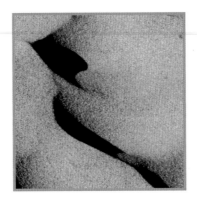

You shape us

    through our experiences.

Icicles glisten
ornamentally.

Your creative embellishments
go beyond necessity.

QUIET GOD

Stately trees are

dusted in stillness.

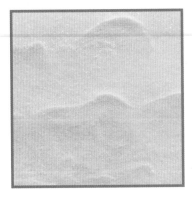

Your quiet embrace

defines us.

Nature offers

winter provisions.

You provide for our needs.

You sustain us.

Velvet snow

   dresses up a winter morning.

You richly clothe us

   with Your blessings.

A clearing offers

a bit of sky and light.

You refresh our spirits

with a glimpse of eternity.

PHOTOGRAPH NOTES

Therese Bach Heyek, B.A. Theology, Cardinal Newman College; Masters in Pastoral Studies, Loyola University Chicago; as a child raised a baby robin in her room until it could fly, as a teenager spent time exploring in nature, as an adult created gardens for schools to bring kids and nature together, and now has joined her love for nature and spirituality in this book. Therese and her husband, Erwin, enjoy being out in nature with their three teenage sons.

Therese welcomes your comments.

www.theresebachheyek.com